SHAKING UP

PROHIBITION

IN NEW ORLEANS

SHAKING UP
PROHIBITION
IN NEW ORLEANS

Authentic Vintage Cocktails from A to Z

**OLIVE LEONHARDT &
HILDA PHELPS HAMMOND**

Drawings by Olive Leonhardt | Edited by Gay Leonhardt

FOREWORD BY JOHN MAGILL

Louisiana State University Press   Baton Rouge

Published by Louisiana State University Press

Copyright © 2015 by Louisiana State University Press

All rights reserved

Manufactured in the United States of America

First printing

Designer: Michelle A. Neustrom
Typeface: Sentinel
Printer and binder: Thomson-Shore, Inc.

Library of Congress Cataloging-in-Publication Data

Leonhardt, Olive, 1895–1963.

    Shaking up prohibition in New Orleans : authentic vintage cocktails from A to Z / Olive Leonhardt and Hilda Phelps Hammond ; drawings by Olive Leonhardt ; edited by Gay Leonhardt.

      pages cm

    ISBN 978-0-8071-5992-7 (cloth : alk. paper) — ISBN 978-0-8071-5993-4 (pdf) — ISBN 978-0-8071-5994-1 (epub) — ISBN 978-0-8071-5995-8 (mobi) 1. Cocktails. I. Hammond, Hilda Phelps, 1890–1951. II. Leonhardt, Gay. III. Title.

    TX951.L455 2014

    641.87′4—dc23

                          2014036420

Portions of John Magill's foreword, "New Orleans during Prohibition: Belligerently Wet," first appeared in different form in "Welcome Old Man Gloom," *Historic New Orleans Collection Newsletter* (Summer 1988), and "Sherwood Anderson in the French Quarter," *Historic New Orleans Collection Newsletter* (Fall 1987).

The paper in this book meets the guidelines for permanence and durability of the Committee on Production Guidelines for Book Longevity of the Council on Library Resources. ♾

for those who continuously enlarge my world:

Olive, Eleanor, and Oliver

CONTENTS

NEW ORLEANS DURING PROHIBITION

Belligerently Wet

The Eighteenth Amendment was passed on October 28, 1919, making illegal the manufacture, sale, and distribution of intoxicating liquor. The term *Prohibition* came from the National Prohibition—or Volstead—Act, which served as the federal police power to carry out the law, and in Louisiana the Hood Act was passed, requiring police to assist federal agents. At the time, a writer using the pseudonym "A. Souse" lamented in the *New Orleans Times-Picayune,* "Gloom, Deep, Dark and Dismal, Descends as Drought Comes." He suggested that people "dig out the sackcloth and ashes, get on the wagon, welcome Old Man Gloom and pretend you like it."

The same newspaper predicted that the "funeral of John Barleycorn promises to be the largest mortuary function in the history of New Orleans," but when the amendment became law on January 16, 1920, the sendoff was anything but boisterous. Criminalization of hard liquor really got underway on June 30, 1919, when the feds reduced allowable alcohol content in liquor, ostensibly to conserve grain. The Crescent City thus slid quietly into one of the most extraordinary—as well as romanticized and glamorized—periods of American history.

New Orleans was hardly fazed by the law. Ferdinand Cowle Iglehart singled the city out in his pro-dry 1919 work *King Alcohol Dethroned* as being under the "saloon's grip," because of its "many foreigners and pleasure loving people." He was not far wrong; in 1929 Sanford Jarrell observed in *New Orleans, the Civilized and Lively City,* "New Orleans is frankly and belligerently wet. It has no sympathy with prohibition and its annual consumption of liquor is appalling." Jarrell concluded, "Hell-bound people have plenty of liquor."

It was probably a year or so after Jarrell's assessment that this book of cocktail recipes, alphabet drawings, and related verse was created. Verse for the letter U mentions stocks going up and down and bulls and bears going round; the market crashed in

October of 1929. The letter L mentions falling hemlines; just days before stocks crashed, the *Times-Picayune* predicted that newer, longer skirts might mean the end of the flapper, and in 1930 hemlines reached the ankles. Could this be a prediction—longer hemlines equal the end of Prohibition? The letter P represents parties. New Orleans loves a good party, and everywhere drinking parties symbolized the roaring twenties—unlike staid balls of earlier generations. In 1930 the novel *Parties,* by Carl Von Vechten—a writer and personality of the drunken twenties—was published.

Liquor commercially manufactured prior to 1920 could legally be consumed, but booze made afterwards was forbidden. There were exceptions, such as liquor acquired at a drugstore for medicinal purposes through a doctor's prescription. The letter R stands for Rx, and a doctor who gave a "neat little / Nice Rx" to his patients. There were limits placed on such "prescriptions," leading G-men in 1925 to charge a number of New Orleans doctors and druggists with abusing the system by issuing and filling prescriptions over the legal limit. Wine was allowed for sacramental use in churches, and in predominantly Roman Catholic New Orleans there were many churches where wine was available. Some, including William Faulkner, got their stash through clergymen—although Faulkner himself claimed to be a rumrunner. This was probably an exaggeration on his part, or untrue. According to Joseph Blotner

in *Faulkner: A Biography,* the best-known French Quarter rumrunner was a man nicknamed Slim who owned a fleet of boats and was said to have studied for the priesthood.

With the amendment's passage, bars instantly became illegal speakeasies, and in New Orleans they were all over town. Jarrell claimed—or boasted—that "the places where alcoholic wines, beer and liquor are sold are too numerous for statistics." Bartenders became cautious about customers, but according to the *New Orleans Item,* "A wink will get you a drink if you're known to the 'house.'"

The letter T stands for "Tst-Tst!" and the "1000 eyes of night"—peepholes in speakeasy doors. Speaks were common in the business district, where they were often called "clubs," befitting a higher and richer class of clientele. One such club, the Stein, was on the second floor of an office building behind a steel door with a peephole. The place was first-class, and the prices were high to keep out "the pikers." The Transportation Club on Common Street served the financial district and was run by an ex-Prohibition agent who knew the ropes. In 1928 seven businessmen's drinking "clubs" were raided for "persistent Volsteadian offenses," according to the *Times-Picayune.* As with many club members, customers known to the bar did not worry about peepholes, since they had their own keys to get in whenever they liked. One well-known speakeasy proprietor was James Brocato, nicknamed

Jimmy Moran, who gained notoriety at midcentury as restaurant owner "Diamond Jim Moran," known for inserting diamonds into meatballs.

In the French Quarter, according to Jarrell, fashionable Uptown ladies "drink cocktails between the acts of Le Petit Théâtre . . . at a frowzy but popular speakeasy around the corner." Also in the Quarter, there were more raffish places like the Picadilly and the Sweet Potato Inn, both on Bienville Street and like many others ultimately padlocked by raids. The Rat's Nest was a dive near Rampart Street that was entered through a small shop and a series of narrow passageways to give access to another house in the rear. "The whiskey served by the one-eyed thug in charge," according to Jarrell, "is the worst I have ever tasted." The lower brands of establishments, where nothing but homemade alcohol was sold to poorer customers, were dubbed "soft drink stands." No matter where, according to Jarrell, "If a cop in uniform drops in for a drink, *he pays for it!*"

"A good percentage of the corner grocers engage in the liquor game on the side," said Jarrell, and his own grocer sold "a very fair brand of wine for $1.40 a gallon . . . and charged like eggs and spinach on the monthly bill." Like any other mom-pop grocery in town, Joe Cassio's, at Royal and St. Peter, did a brisk business in liquor—even if it was not of the best quality.

Restaurants never stopped serving drinks, and Jarrell wrote that "if one is known, one may enjoy wine either imported or domestic, and top off the dinner with a liqueur." There were instances of waiters serving drinks from hip flasks, and euphemisms were coined, such as "small blacks"—booze served in demitasses with mixers on the side. Elegant and fabled Antoine's on St. Louis Street stashed its fine wine and liquor in a separate building around the corner—as did other restaurants—to minimize alcohol in the dining room for quick disposal in case of a raid. Antoine's had the Mystery Room—a backroom speakeasy—entered by way of the ladies' restroom. Arnaud's Restaurant was raided, and owner Count Arnaud went to jail. Even the venerable private Boston Club was raided—no arrests, but one hundred bottles of the best wines and liquors were seized.

New Orleans was one of America's most exotic cities, particularly the picturesque French Quarter, and in the 1920s a number of writers and artists moved there for creative inspiration. Novelist Sherwood Anderson, who arrived in 1922, proclaimed New Orleans the most civilized place in America. He found the population to be "charmingly unambitious, basically cultured and gentle." He concluded that their love of leisure was synonymous with culture; thus New Orleans was "the most cultured city I had yet found in America." Another writer, Oliver La Farge, said that in the mid-1920s he and his friends in the Quarter could do much as they pleased without scandalizing the neighbors.

At the start of Prohibition, artist William Spratling bought ten large jugs of absinthe—which itself had been illegal in the United States since 1912—from a bootlegger to share with his friends. Sherwood Anderson wrote to Gertrude Stein that "there is little prohibition here[;] everyone is properly gay and at least half abandoned to fun." Anderson's wife Elizabeth recalled that there was a great deal of drinking in their literary crowd, but "little drunkenness. We all seemed to feel that Prohibition was a personal affront and that we had a moral duty to undermine it."

In this book, the letter C stands for newspaper columnists. The drawing alludes to the writers Walter Winchell—whose column was subtitled "Things I Never Knew 'til Now" and who was a friend of New York gangster Owney Madden—Heywood Broun, and O. O. McIntyre, all providing America with their take on Prohibition. These columnists are said to be "Under One Sheet at the Morgue," likely the New Orleans morgue, where local newspaper writers—most of whom were part of the French Quarter literary crowd—stashed their beer in refrigerated surroundings.

The public drinking that has long been part of life in New Orleans was not dampened by Prohibition. One conspicuous entrepreneur tootled an automobile around downtown streets selling drinks at curbside. On holidays like Christmas and New Year's Eve, people thronged the streets, many of them openly drinking. At Mardi Gras this was especially true, with Jarrell writing, "If I may be permitted to say so, a majority of the adults [are] in various stages of intoxication. The lid is off for Mardi Gras. Even the prohibition agents keep to their kennels. The revelers don't go in for hip flasks . . . they tilt quart bottles to their lips."

With a long history as an essential port, and a wholesale distribution center for imported wines and liquors, New Orleans quickly became one of Prohibition's leading rum-running destinations. The long coastline with many inlets and bayous near the city provided a shield for rumrunners. At first, foreign liquor was smuggled in via Lake Pontchartrain, but then activity shifted to St. Bernard Parish and then Barataria. Aiding smugglers was considered a legitimate way to supplement income and became a way of life for many families. Ships were met by oyster luggers and pleasure boats that took the booze ashore. Armed gunmen escorted trucks into the city for further distribution. This illicit trade was no secret, and frequently one could go fishing and buy liquor straight off the boat from a fisherman in the marshes.

In spite of Louisiana's Hood Act, local police did little to cooperate with federal agencies—and actually had little motivation to do so, since pay was so low. Some police worked with bootleggers. While Prohibition-era New Orleans had its share of underworld bootleggers, smugglers, lawbreakers, and gunfights, they tended to fly under the radar, since none gained the national notoriety of gangs like Al Capone's in Chicago. New Orleans was not big enough to absorb all of the liquor being brought in, but as a distribution center it sent a good deal north and some of the booze did end up in Capone's Chicago operation. Truckloads of liquor labeled as canned fruit from Kenner—then a farm town—went to the Windy City, according to Louis Vyhnanek in *Unorganized Crime: New Orleans in the 1920s,* and to one of Capone's speakeasies, where raids linked the supply to Crescent City bootleggers.

Local attitudes about the Eighteenth Amendment were verified by federal agent Izzy Einstein, who was noted for his ability to track down lawbreakers. Often in disguise for his detective work, he was followed by the press like a celebrity. He went to New Orleans in 1923 on a nationwide search to uncover the city with the easiest access to liquor. The *Item* featured the portly Einstein puffing his cigar on the front page as it would any visiting movie star or foreign dignitary. Einstein arrived at one of the city's railroad stations, hailed a taxi, and asked the driver where he could score a drink. Instead of taking him to a speakeasy, the driver offered him a bottle pulled from under the seat. Total time 35 seconds—New Orleans won the contest.

Too undermanned to adequately enforce the law, feds generally did not bother home violators, but raids against bigger lawbreakers such as speak-easies, restaurants, bootleggers, and stills were frequent. Breweries met trouble for making illegal real beer, and several large stills operated, giving their owners the "stature of Capone," in the words of the S verse.

The area's largest mass crackdown happened on August 11, 1925, when two hundred out-of-town agents assisted in a series of sensational raids that aimed to clean up the city. Thousands of crates of seized liquor filled the halls and offices of local federal headquarters at the U.S. Custom House on Canal Street. G-men marveled at the extraordinary amounts of liquor confiscated as one speak-easy after another was hit. In spite of the enormous amount of seized alcohol, one bootlegger was unmoved, telling the *Times-Picayune* that the feds "didn't get such an awful amount. I don't believe the price of liquor in New Orleans will go up—much."

Still, there were changes in the air. The *Times-Picayune* reported, "The 'be careful' went out last night along the Tango Belt." The only customers being let into speakeasies were the "safe" ones known to the bartender. A major fatality of the get-tough attitude was the Tango Belt. This was an area of saloons, honky-tonks, and dance halls in and around Iberville Street known for partying and nightlife since the early twentieth century. Raids killed the Tango Belt's business, and by the time Prohibition was repealed in 1933, Bourbon Street was becoming the new center of French Quarter nightclubs.

Beginning in 1926, there was a growing tendency on the part of feds across the country to not just fine and release lawbreakers, but to jail the perpetrators and padlock speakeasies. Prior to this, most arrested barkeepers paid fines and reopened their bars. Padlocking for an extended time put speakeasies out of business. In New Orleans—one of the wettest cities in the country—federal agents were on a mission with the slogan, "Let's close 'em up by New Year's." The *Item* reported that in December 1926, 86 bars were padlocked in New Orleans. In 1927 it was estimated that the city had more padlocked speakeasies than any other place in the nation.

At the beginning of Prohibition, smuggled foreign brands, which were generally safe and of high quality, were readily available in New Orleans. The growing activity of the federal government, with raids by the coast guard and arrests by customs agents, helped curtail this trade and brought about an increase in moonshine and adulterated alcohol, which could be contaminated and even lethal. As speakeasies were padlocked, home drinking increased.

Families were allowed to make a limited amount of wine, although many went beyond the legal limit and some made more than just wine. From the start, many people in New Orleans turned to making home brew. Recipes and outfits for making beer were available, along with ingredients like malt and hops, from retailers such as the New Orleans Hops, Malt and Extracts Company, which had several locations. Soon after Prohibition started, an estimated 10,000 people in New Orleans were already lawbreakers. Verse for the letter F implies that a family drinking together stays together. By the late twenties there was even more brew made at home, because of raids and shutdowns. The letter U refers to undertakers kept busy, probably caused by the increase in toxic bathtub liquor. The letter M stands, among other things, for milk of magnesia, a product for settling an upset stomach probably brought on by too much bad booze.

Finally in 1933, as the country wallowed in the depths of the Great Depression, Congress enacted a law allowing Americans to buy beer containing 3.2 percent alcohol. Over the space of just a few days, 911 retail beer permits were issued in New Orleans. Restaurants and hotels opened beer gardens, where customers did not have to sneak their beer from under the table.

At noon on April 13, 1933, as the law went into effect, sirens wailed, Canal Street filled with cheering celebrants, and the *Times-Picayune* reported that "there had not been so spontaneous an outpouring of joyous citizenry since the Armistice." Convoys of beer trucks filed down streets, and in the short space of a few hours 488,000 gallons of beer had been sold to bars—about one gallon for each man, woman, and child living in the city. The *Times-Picayune* enthused, "New Orleans can have a jubilant legal whoopee party . . . the skyscrapers will be a-rocking and a-reeling before midnight."

Prohibition was repealed by the Twenty-first Amendment, which went into effect on December 5, 1933. Hard liquor was now legal again. The jubilant outpouring to celebrate the death of the Eighteenth Amendment was not repeated in New Orleans, and the city quietly passed into a new post-Prohibition world. One barkeeper summed it up to the *Times-Picayune,* saying, "We've been selling everything for the past few weeks, why should anyone get excited over official repeal?" The newspaper perhaps best assessed the local reaction to the demise of Prohibition when it commented, "For the first time in the past 13 years, the lights were turned out in one of the city's leading French restaurants as café bruleau [*sic*] was prepared before an admiring group of patrons."

—John Magill

SOURCES

Anderson, Elizabeth, and Gerald R. Kelly. *Miss Elizabeth: A Memoir.* Boston: Little, Brown, 1969.

Anderson, Sherwood. *Sherwood Anderson's Memoirs.* New York: Harcourt, Brace, 1942.

———. *Sherwood Anderson's Notebook: Containing Articles Written during the Author's Life as a Story Teller, and Notes from Life Scattered through the Book.* New York: Boni and Liveright, 1926.

Blotner, Joseph. *Faulkner: A Biography.* 2 vols. New York: Random House, 1974.

Iglehart, Ferdinand Cowle. *King Alcohol Dethroned.* Westerville, Ohio: American Issue Pub. Co., 1919.

Jarrell, Sanford. *New Orleans, the Civilized and Lively City.* Girard, Kans.: Haldeman-Julius Pubs., 1929.

Jones, Howard Mumford, and Walter B. Rideout, eds. *Letters of Sherwood Anderson.* Boston: Little, Brown, 1953.

Kobler, John. *Ardent Spirits: The Rise and Fall of Prohibition.* New York: Putnam, 1973.

Modlin, Charles E., ed., *Sherwood Anderson: Selected Letters.* Knoxville: University of Tennessee Press, 1984.

New Orleans Item. Jan. 16, Apr. 25, 1920; Nov. 21, 1923; July 14, 15, 1924; Aug. 11, 1925; Dec. 10, 1926.

New Orleans States, Nov. 13, 1921.

New Orleans Times-Picayune, June 30, July 1, Oct. 28, 29, 1919; May 15, 1920; June 26, 29, 1921; May 17, July 14, 15, 1924; Aug. 12, 1925; Apr 13, 14, Dec. 6, 1933.

Okrent, Daniel. *Last Call: The Rise and Fall of Prohibition.* New York: Scribner, 2010.

Pitts, Stella. "The Quarter in the Twenties." *New Orleans Times-Picayune,* Nov. 26, 1972.

Sutton, William A., ed. *Letters to Bab: Sherwood Anderson to Marietta D. Finley, 1916–33* Urbana: University of Illinois Press, 1985.

Taylor, Welford Dunaway. *Sherwood Anderson.* New York: Ungar, 1977.

Vyhnanek, Louis. *Unorganized Crime: New Orleans in the 1920s.* Lafayette, La.: Center for Louisiana Studies, 1998.

White, Ray Lewis, ed. *Sherwood Anderson/Gertrude Stein: Correspondence and Personal Essays.* Chapel Hill: University of North Carolina Press, 1972.

THE ONGOING JOKE

Olive Leonhardt and Hilda Phelps Hammond during Prohibition

Olive Ellzey Leonhardt, my grandmother, was an artist. She died in 1963 when I was twelve. I only met her once. All her work was left in her studio in her home on Pitt Street in New Orleans. When her husband died in 1978, the house was sold and its possessions divvied up among family. I was an artist myself by this point, and I was intrigued by her work. After relatives took a few oils, I had all her remaining art, correspondence, and papers shipped north, where they sat in storage for thirty years while I raised a family and pursued my own career.

Eight years ago, I moved Olive's work to my basement. A flood in my finished basement caused a panicked removal of her art from its boxes. For weeks I had all her oils leaning against the walls of my house. The range of subject matter was fascinating: a caesarian section, a portrait of a clown, a stylized Mexican street scene, two figures in a tomb, a series composed in a stained-glass motif, portraits of people she knew, and more. Through living with her art in this odd way I decided to learn more about Olive. I read through her papers. I sorted through the many portfolios with the idea of getting some recognition for her work. Olive had showed extensively in her hometown of New Orleans during her lifetime, and she had a one-woman show in New York City in 1939. She mysteriously turned down requests from both the Museum of Modern Art and the Whitney Museum of American Art to review her work. Yet she is now quite obscure.

I came upon the typescript for this book among Olive's many portfolios. The drawing style immediately caught my eye; it was unlike that of her other drawings or pastels. Olive's fine art from that period was primarily strong representational line drawing or fully shaded portraits done in graphite. These illustrations were pen and ink with a bold graphic style.

The typescript was titled "Letters from a Shaker." It had a cover page written in pencil in block letters, saying the text was by Olive and Hilda Phelps Hammond. That cover page with its paper clips rusted into the paper was the only documentation of their joint project. While I had learned a great deal about Olive's life, I knew little about Hilda.

Y

A year and a half into Prohibition, several women in a shop in New Orleans were looking at trophies for an upcoming horse show. A riding stick caught the attention of one woman. She asked, "Tell me, is that one of those sticks with a flask in it?" Another replied, "How times have changed. Once, it was the drink that had the stick in it; and now it's the stick that has the drink in it."[1]

Natalie Scott, who wrote that story in her gossip column, taught at Newcomb High School when Olive entered for her junior year. They became friends. Hilda Phelps was Natalie's best friend.

Hilda had been born in 1890, five years before Olive. Hilda's father was a New Orleans newspaper publisher, and her mother had attended Sophie Newcomb College. Hilda grew up as a privileged debutante and a queen of Mardi Gras. She was president of her graduating class at Newcomb, a star in dramatics, and a prizewinner in debating. She also had a master's degree in English from Tulane University.

This was a far cry from my grandmother's background. Her family had been tainted by scandal. Olive's father was a disgraced businessman who had deserted his family in McComb, Mississippi, to run off with a young second cousin. He was murdered by a posse in Texas when Olive was six. Olive and her mother moved to New Orleans around 1910. How they managed financially is unclear. Her mother was a woman of old southern values, more acquainted with crocheting than education. Olive went to Newcomb, not for a quality liberal arts education as Hilda did, but to study art and learn a profession. She attended the New York School of Fine and Applied Arts (later to become Parsons School of Design) for a year before getting a job doing graphics at the D. H. Holmes department store on Canal Street.

Olive and Hilda worked together in the New Orleans suffrage movement. In the 1920s they socialized (often with Natalie Scott), played bridge together, and were both involved in the Junior League from its formation in New Orleans. Olive created the cover for the program of the 1925 Junior League fundraising theatrical event and made posters. Hilda chaired the publicity committee and did advertising.

Olive and Hilda probably produced this book in late 1929 or early 1930. This surmise is based on references in the poems to falling skirt lengths and the pun "does behoove her," written as "beHoover," in the verse for letter A.

By 1930 both women were married with children. Olive's art had been all over town. In the early 1920s

Hilda in 1925. Photo appeared in Junior League booklet for that year.

Junior League Revue (March 1925): 6. Ephemera Collection, Louisiana Research Collection, Tulane University.

Olive, circa 1925.

Collection of Gay Leonhardt.

she had designed covers for *The Double Dealer,* a literary magazine that published the first Faulkner and Hemingway, and illustrations for newspaper articles. She had created sets for Le Petit Théâtre and posters for events such as a visiting show of Rookwood pottery, and horse shows. She had also joined the Arts and Crafts Club (a gallery space and art school in the French Quarter) in its first year and created promotional art for its annual balls.

Beginning in 1921, Olive had a studio in the French Quarter with two other regularly showing local artists, Caroline Durieux and Fanny Craig. In

1926 Olive studied for a summer at the Art Students' League in New York City, after which she started showing oils in exhibits at the Arts and Crafts Club. She also traveled alone to Europe in the twenties to sketch at the great sites and museums. In 1930 Olive was one of many honored at the prestigious Orleans Club for her contributions to the arts in New Orleans. Her paintings were also accepted in juried shows that brought her art to Danville, Virginia, and the Cincinnati Art Museum. She signed most of her illustrative work with "Leon" and her fine art with "Olive Leonhardt."

The ink illustrations for this book were done on heavy, 9 × 12 1/2 Strathmore drawing boards. The illustrations are full of spinning, falling, and swirling images to suggest drunkenness. Unlike the diversity of styles in her fine art drawings, Olive maintained one particular look for the book, just as she had done for the covers of *The Double Dealer*.

Despite their differences in upbringing and class, Olive and Hilda were both known for being independent and outspoken. Both women rejected the societal standards of behavior for young matrons. One of Hilda's daughters said of her mother, "She didn't cook, she didn't sew, she didn't garden."[2] Hilda was a natural leader. Olive had a reputation for traveling to remote areas alone. A friend, Evelyn Witherspoon, said about her, "She did what she wanted to do and she was a person who was driven by her own."[3] Olive thought nothing of building a brick wall in her backyard by herself. She socialized with both the country club women and the bohemian French Quarter set.

Olive had a salon at her Uptown house in the 1920s. She regularly invited artists and writers such as Bill Spratling, Natalie Scott, James Feibleman, Charles Bein, Weeks Hall, and Lyle Saxon for drinks, dinner, and talk. Hilda attended prominent Mardi Gras balls and parties famous for their culture of drinking. She socialized with the elite class in New Orleans. Though Hilda had a more extensive formal education, both women were well read and spoke French fluently. Their classical educations are reflected in the language of the poems and recipe titles. Words such as *callithump, wamble, quidnunc,* and *vivandière* require glossing for a modern reader.

Hilda's comfortable life changed dramatically when Huey Long fired her husband in March 1930. Despite having practiced for years as a lawyer, he found it hard to get work due to the Long political machine and the Depression. Hilda began writing cooking articles for the *Times Picayune*. She wrote, "The ten-dollar bill which I received each week in return for the culinary triumphs on the market basket page filled in many of the widening cracks of hard times."[4] Since she didn't cook, she got recipes from friends and wrote stories about the dishes.

Natalie Scott published a cookbook in 1929. Olive did the cover. Natalie included a recipe for an after-dinner drink, "Café Brulot," made with coffee, spices, and brandy. Natalie dealt with the issue of Prohibition by including this note: "This—no longer possible, of course (?)—is a cherished old after-dinner tradition, dear to memory."[5] With recipes so much a part of their lives, it's not surprising that Olive and Hilda decided to make an alphabet cocktail recipe book with a text that made fun of drinking, not drinking, and Prohibition.

Prohibition was a joke in their world. Accounts from every source indicate that their New Orleans remained a drinking city during Prohibition. Edmund Wilson even listed some of the drinks he had during a visit in 1926: beer, absinthe frappés, Sazerac cocktails, scotch, curaçao, and particular wines.[6] Large costume balls given for *The Double Dealer* and the Arts and Crafts Club in the twenties always included alcohol. Hilda and Olive could get drinks at restaurants, clubs, bars, and private homes. Natalie Scott called the cocktails at a downtown restaurant "New Orleans Volsteads."[7]

This book is a curious historical document. I doubt Olive and Hilda intended to publish a collection of cocktail recipes during Prohibition. The text makes fun of both prohibiting alcohol and drunken behavior, avoiding any polemic tone. It scoffs at doctors prescribing alcohol, drinking games, speakeasies, hangovers, homemade brew, and social norms. The "Apodosis" gives advice for hostesses. The diversity of the cocktail recipes requires a well-stocked bar.

The text was certainly put together before 1933, when Hilda began attending the U.S. Senate committee meetings to investigate voter fraud in the election of Senator John Overton, Long's hand-picked candidate. Her indignation at the failure of the Senate to act led her to form the Women's Committee of Louisiana, which instituted an intensive nationwide letter-writing campaign. She visited Washington, D.C., repeatedly over two years in her efforts to persuade the Senate of the political corruption in Louisiana. Hilda wrote an account of her anti-Long activities in *Let Freedom Ring* (1936). She was involved with the League of Women Voters and had a political radio show in the 1940s. She died in 1951.

Olive had a book of her drawings called *New Orleans: Drawn and Quartered* published in 1938, had a one-woman show at the Charles Morgan Gallery in New York in 1939, and showed regularly in New Orleans during the forties. She turned to abstract art in the fifties. She died in 1963.

Each of the original illustrations has thumbtack holes at the top corners. Perhaps Hilda and Olive put the drawings up and wrote their verse to the illustrations. I'd like to think that they had a party and displayed the drawings while they read the text. The guests would have been offered "olives wrapped in bacon," "weenie sandwiches [that] are piping," and cocktails.

—Gay Leonhardt

NOTES

1. *New Orleans States,* July 3, 1921, 36.

2. Pamela Tyler, *Silk Stockings and Ballot Boxes: Women and Politics in New Orleans, 1920–1963* (Athens: University of Georgia Press, 1996), 64.

3. Interview with Evelyn Witherspoon, 1982.

4. Hilda Phelps Hammond, *Let Freedom Ring* (New York: Farrar & Rinehart, 1936), 46.

5. Natalie Scott, *Mirations and Miracles of Mandy: Some Favorite Louisiana Recipes* (New Orleans: R. H. True, 1929), 61.

6. Edmund Wilson, *The Twenties* (New York: Farrar, Straus & Giroux, 1975), 251–53.

7. John W. Scott, *Natalie Scott: A Magnificent Life* (Gretna, La.: Pelican Publishing Co., 2008), 239.

A NOTE ON THE TEXT & THE RECIPES

The text here is presented in close imitation of the original typescript, which was entitled "Letters from a Shaker." There may be some typographical errors in the original. Some misspellings exist but are easily understood.

The cocktail recipes seem to be a combination of slightly reformulated standard cocktails, old drinks, and the authors' creations. For example, the Fribble is a Mary Pickford (a cocktail named for the 1920s movie star), the Statiscope resembles a Clover Club, and the Black Jack is a Stinger.

"Hydropot Exterminator" is clearly meant as a joke. The recipe at "M" for milk of magnesia and castor oil should be taken with a grain of salt. It is untested. Otherwise, all recipes are intended for consumption. A few of the recipes, such as Q.E.D., have fractional components that do not add up to a whole, or add up to more than one. The reader should feel free to experiment with these. The measurement "a glass of" generally referred to a 2-ounce glass at the time these recipes were written down, though by the 1930s it could also be 4 ounces. With the exception of lithia water, all the ingredients are available. Any other particulars about the cocktails are footnoted.

SHAKING UP
PROHIBITION
IN NEW ORLEANS

PROEM[*]

Drymen's
Abstinence and Abitafull.[†]

> In recent times, ere gunmen did begin,
> Before potations deep were made a sin
> When man on many multiplied his kind
> Ere one to one was legally confined
> Came all the Antis-
> Wide was their command
> Scattering their wishes in and out the land.
>
> Not in the pay of Wets or Drys are we
> (As from these pages you will quickly see)
> Yet can we not refrain from giving praise
> To all the wonders of these happy days.
> What benefits we constantly perceive
> More than we dared to hope or dared believe!

---

[*] proem: a prelude, a preamble.

[†] "Drymen's Abstinence and Abitafull" is a parody of John Dryden's famous poem "Absalom and Achitophel," dated 1681. It begins: "In pious times, ere priest-craft did begin, / Before polygamy was made a sin; / When man on many multiplied his kind, / Ere one to one was cursedly confined. . . ."

2.

How lovely life has daily waxed and grown
    Since The Amendment has to all been known!
What splendid bounteous hospitality
    In every state and each locality,
How soft the voices, clear and cool
    Since speaking easy is the rule.

What courage, rivalling that of Sparta,
    Is shown by those who buy and barter,
How many heroes strut the street
    Gay Buccaneers, caponely neat.
E'en medicine has preened itself
    Prescriptions flanking every shelf.

How laudable is the advancing
    Of all the arts—especially dancing,
Uplifted are the minds artistic
    With Thurber drawings realistic
Charming the family circle too
    With home the centre of home brew.

3.

Even the alphabet's acquired
A novel meaning for the tired
    And shades of Puritans and Quakers
Send messages from silent shakers.
    When evening's clouds begin to lower
Then comes the gentle cocktail hour
    And children, at their parents' knees
Do learn their letters with much ease,
    Absorbing culture, so refining
From every shaker's silver lining.

These blessings we do not perceive
More than we dared to hope or dared believe!

Old Uncle Sam has now a wife
 He says he's wedded her for life,
But in a delicate condition
 We find poor Auntie Prohibition.
Her stepson Scotch, her stepson Rye,
 Have thrived beneath her watchful eye
Her foster children (wine and beer)
 Quite full of spirits do appear!
While her own darling, Homemade Gin
 Is better than it's ever been.
Yet though her offspring wax and thrive
 Poor Auntie scarcely seems alive,
Soon to the grave must Sam remove her
 With dignity as does beHoover!*

AIR MINDED

2/3 Absinthe
1/6 Gin
1/6 Syrup of Annisette
1 Touch of Angostura
1 Touch of Orange

ALLEZ-OOP†

3/8 French Vermouth
1/2 Apple Jack
1/8 Grenadine
Juice of 1/2 Lemon
Few Absinthe Drops

---

* "beHoover": a reference to Herbert Hoover, president 1929–33. † "Allez-Oop": the cry of a circus acrobat about to leap.

The bottle always used to be
 The necromancer's[*] agency.
Magicians' wands drew eggs and rabbits
 From bottles for the gaping Babbits.[†]
But what magicians erstwhile drew
 Is nothing to what I and you
Can get from out a bottle fragile
 When it's uncorked by fingers agile.
What neck romancy's brought to light
 What apparitions fiercely bright,
What tricks can I (and also You)
 Upon a single bottle do!

BLACK JACK

1/2 White Mint[‡]
1/2 Cognac

BASHI-BAZOUK[§]

1/3 Bacardi Rum
2/3 Brandy
1 Dash lemon juice
1 Teaspoon Grenadine

---

[*] necromancer: one who performs magic or divination through communicating with the dead.

[†] Babbits: Sinclair Lewis's book *Babbitt* was published in 1922. To be a Babbitt is to be a conforming, middle-class fool.

[‡] White Mint: clear crème de menthe.

[§] bashi-bazouk: irregular mounted soldier in the Turkish military, or an undisciplined person.

Cracks both wise and otherwise
    Make us titter with surprise.
Things you never knew before
    Things I never heard or saw!
Every man though blithe or solemn
    Does his little daily column.[*]
Every buzz is welcome grist
    For the key hole humorist,
What a jocose people we
    Since the nation's F.F.V!

F. F.V. = Fastidious For Volstead.

CALLITHUMP[†]

1/6 Gin
1/6 Glass Kirsch
1/6 Glass Maraschino
1/6 Curacoa[‡]
1/6 French Vermouth
1/6 Italian Vermouth

CELLOPHANE

1/2 Sloe Gin
1/2 Apple Jack

Things you never knew 'till now!

---

[*] Of those noted in the drawing opposite, Walter Winchell was a gossip columnist for the *New York Daily Mirror* and later a radio show host. Heywood Broun and O. O. McIntyre were humorous columnists who wrote against Prohibition.

[†] callithump: a riotous, noisy parade.
[‡] Curacoa: usually spelled "Curacao." Orange curaçao.

D is Delirium
    Tremens and twitter,
Bacchantean blossom
    Sapidity* bitter!
The wamble,† the waggle
    The serpentine teeter
That loosens the limbos
    And unseats the seater!

DAHABEAH‡

1/4 Curacao
1/4 Yellow Chartreuse
1/4 Annisette
1/4 Brandy

*(This is guaranteed to furnish all the sensations of a
Dahabeah adorned with rhythm women.)*

---

* sapidity: a good flavor; the quality of being savory.
† wamble: to move unsteadily, or to feel nauseous.

‡ dahabeah: a passenger boat on the Nile.

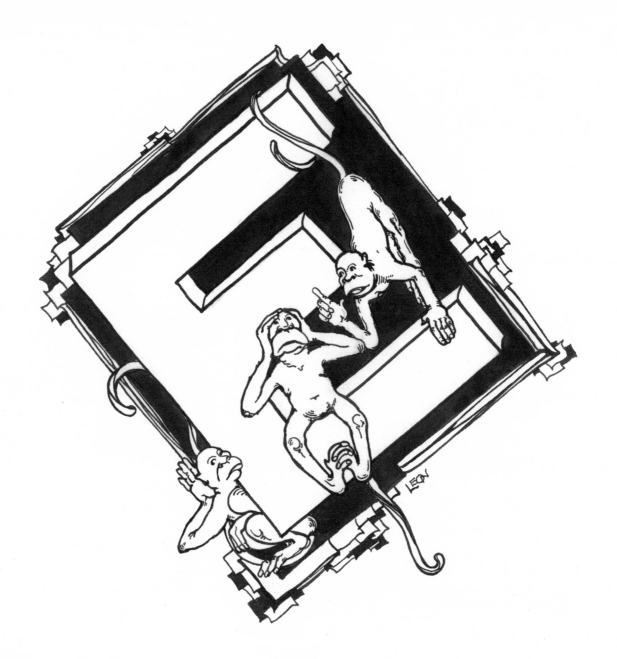

E is the Earful
    That all of us get
Whenever we're cheerful
    Convivial and wet.
But the earfuls of wets
    Are considerably better
Than the earfuls of drys
    Who must wish they were wetter!

ESCALATOR

1/3 Rye Whiskey
1/3 Port Wine
White of a fresh egg
Juice of 1/2 lemon
1 Teaspoon sugar

EAR MUFFLER

1/4 French Vermouth
1/4 Italian Vermouth
1/2 Swedish Punch*

Not a step in a carload!

---

* Swedish Punch: a liqueur containing arrack.

Behold the blessed Family life
 Relaxed and easy, free from strife!
Father has his rock and rye
 Mother takes her cocktail dry,
Brother drinks his corn and gin
 Sister pours the liquor in,
Every friend drops in that passes
 Baby licks from all the glasses!
Family life so triply blest
 With happy parent, child and guest!

FRIBBLE*

1/8 Grenadine
2/8 Pineapple Juice
5/8 Bacardi rum

FORTISSIMO

1/3 Creme de Cacao
1/3 Apricot Brandy
Garnish on top with
whipped cream

---

*fribble: to act in a foolish or frivolous manner, or to falter or totter.

Gay Gymnastics once again
  Seize the ladies and the men.
Morning, evening, noon and night
  Parlor, bath or penthouse sight.
Figures that can never lie
  Comfortably until they die,
Bend in two and rise once more,
  Hips Hoorah upon the floor.
Waist not, want not goes the saw
  Pounds run up on whiskey raw
Hence the bending maids and mannies,
  Not for them the buxom Fannies!

GEMINI

1/2 Gin
1/2 French Vermouth

GYROSCOPE

1/3 Rye Whiskey
1/3 Orange Juice
1/3 Lemon Juice

Instead of shaking turn round and round.

H is the Hydropot*
　　Looking for what we've not.
Wanly he seeks the brink
　　Of running brook to drink,
Scotch, Rye and corking rum
　　Cocktails—these make him glum
Poor, solitary person
　　There is a sober curse on
Him—he will die forgot,
　　Unhappy Hydropot!

HYDROPOT EXTERMINATOR

1 bottle White Rock†
1, 2 or 3 dashes of arsenic
1 pinch
Works rapidly—they leave the house
and die in the open. No odor.

---

*hydropot: a water drinker or a teetotaler.　　　　　†White Rock: brand name for a type of seltzer.

I's Introspection
    So new and so chic,
Just a trio of highballs
    Will make us all peek
Into things that we never
    Imagined we would,
And reflect upon others
    That we doubt if we should!

IO*

Juice of 1/2 Lemon
1/2 Tablespoon of Powdered Sugar
White of 1 Egg
1 Glass Dry Gin†
3 Dashes Orange Flower Water
2 Tablespoons of Sweet Cream

---

*Io: one of the four largest moons of Jupiter.   †1 glass: 2 to 4 oz.

Jitters one can best express
   In jabbering words of emptiness,
Birdie witted, episodic
   Also tant soit peu nomadic,[*]
Paracme[†] to every smile,
   Rococo but so worth while!

JUJUBE

1 Teaspoon of Sugar
4 Dashes Angostura Bitters
1 Teaspoon Lemon Juice
1 Glass of Gin
Ice

JABBERNOWL[‡]

(un sot a triple etage[§])
1/3 French Vermouth
1/3 Italian Vermouth
2/3 Angostura Bitters

---

[*] "tant soit peu nomadic": slightly nomadic or slightly aimless.
[†] paracme: the time after a crisis of fever when the symptoms improve.

[‡] "jabbernowl": an alternate spelling for "jobbernowl," or stupid person.
[§] "un sot à triple étage": literally, "a fool to the third story"—a blockhead.

K is the Knockout
That Everyone gets
　Without any ring seats
Without any bets.
　No need to pay prices
That worry and pinch
　When every good couple
Can go in a clinch.
　No need to strain eyesight
And hearts at the fight
　When a Knockout is yours
Just any old night!

KALSOMINE* PUNCH

1/2 Pound of Powdered Sugar
2 Quarts Champagne
1 Quart Sparkling Mineral Water
1 Glass Brandy
1 Glass Maraschino
1 Glass Curacao
Pour over slab of ice in which
seasonable fruit has been frozen.

---

*kalsomine: a whitewash that is an inexpensive paint.

The Lady who was passing fast
    B.P.* now is saved at last!
No more the skirts above the knee
    No more the fulsome figure free,
Back are the harnesses of steel
    Down are the dresses to the heel
Each damsel now is sure to notice
    To cover up her apodosis.†
Oh Lady, just about to pass
    We've found you in an A.P. glass!

LACKADAISY

1/4 Part Gin

1/4 Part Benedictine

1/4 Part Lemon

1/4 Part Lithia Water‡

LAH-DA-DA

1 Teaspoon Raspberry Syrup

1 Teaspoon Lemon Juice

2/3 Gin

1 Dash Maraschino

---

* "B.P." and "A.P" might mean "Before Prohibition" and "After Prohibition."

† apodosis: the main clause of a conditional sentence. Used here to mean buttocks.

‡ lithia water: a popular soda water containing lithium salts that is no longer available. Substitute any seltzer.

Gaze upon the Milky way
Heavenly path that blots out day,
    Sometimes many stars you see
Sometimes only 1, 2, 3
    Backed by Mr. Hennessy.

Galaxy of astral bodies,
Clearly seen just after toddies,
    To this earth at break of day
Comes a welcome Milky Way
    Good for any astral seizure
Gentle, helpful, pure
    Magnesia.

MORE MARGIN

(Don't gag)
1/3 Castor Oil
2/3 Milk of Magnesia
1 dash bitters to cover—
Stir with ticker tape.

Nittennotten makes us be
　　Scintillating company,
Let us nit or let us not
　　Says the hostess on the spot,
Crack a you—the murder game,
　　Anagrams in case you're lame,
Or numerica[*] perhaps
　　(John T's[†] scientific craps)
Jig saw puzzles piece by piece
　　Help our thyroids to increase,
Lot's old rib just plain forgot
　　'Cause she never nittennot!

NODDY[‡]

1　Teaspoon Lime Juice
2/3　Rum
1/3　Sherry

NITTENNOT

2/3　Creme de Cacao
1/6　Fresh Cream

---

[*] Numerica: a Parker Brothers board game introduced in 1894.

[†] "John T." is likely to be a typographical error. John D. Rockefeller was known to be an avid player of Numerica, often playing after every meal.

[‡] noddy: a sixteenth-century English card game.

In drawing opposite: "Johnny Jump Up" is a cocktail of apple cider with a shot of whiskey and also the name of a flower, the viola.

O for Orations
That Bibuli* spout,
   The more that goes in
The more then comes out!
   The shade of Demosthenese
Cowers with shame
   When the modern carouser
Begins to declaim.

OYEZ!†

1/2 Gordon's Gin
1/2 Bols Kummel‡

O-OH-HUM

1 Dash Absinthe
1/6 Grenadine
1/6 Vodka
1/3 Orange Juice
1/3 Gin

---

*bibuli: plural form of "bibulo" (one who is fond of drinking).
†"Oyez!": an interjection used to open a law court.

‡Kummel: a liqueur, first distilled by Hans Bols.

Parties!
Parties, Parties, Parties
Parties, Parties, Parties, Parties, Parties
Parties, Parties, Parties
Parties!
Parties, Parties, Parties
Parties, Parties, Parties, Parties, Parties
Parties, Parties, Parties
Parties!

PROPELLER

1/2 Gin
1/2 Italian Vermouth

PERISCOPE

1/4 Orange Juice
1/2 Gin
1/8 French Vermouth
1/8 Italian Vermouth

The Quaint little Quidnunc,[*]
   Society's Moppet,[†]
Asks questions unending
   Not once does he stop it!
He whensies and wheresies
   And howmuchis each bottle,
And his cute little queries
   Nobody can throttle.

Q.E.D.[‡]

2/3 White Creme de Menthe
1/2 Brandy

QUIDNUNC

4 Glasses of Sherry
1 Glass Whiskey
1 Glass Rum
1 Glass Pure Syrup
Dash of Orange Bitters
A little Simple Syrup

---

[*] quidnunc: a gossip who is constantly saying, "What now?"
[†] moppet: English word for "child," or a contemptuous reference to a frivolous woman.

[‡] Q.E.D.: a phrase put at the end of a mathematical proof, standing for "quod erat demonstrandum."

There once was a popular
   Old M.D.
Who had more patients
   Than he could see.

Some had the quinzy
   Some had the gout
And some had things
   They couldn't talk about.

But he gave each man
   For his sad affliction
The same little, neat little
   Nice Rx

And They didn't have quinzy
   They didn't have gout
But they all had something
   They could talk about.

RUMBA

1 Glass Dubonnet
1/2 Glass Syrup Citron*
Balance Soda Water

REMOTE CONTROL

1/3 Kummel
2/3 Brandy

---

* syrup citron: a nonalcoholic lemon syrup.

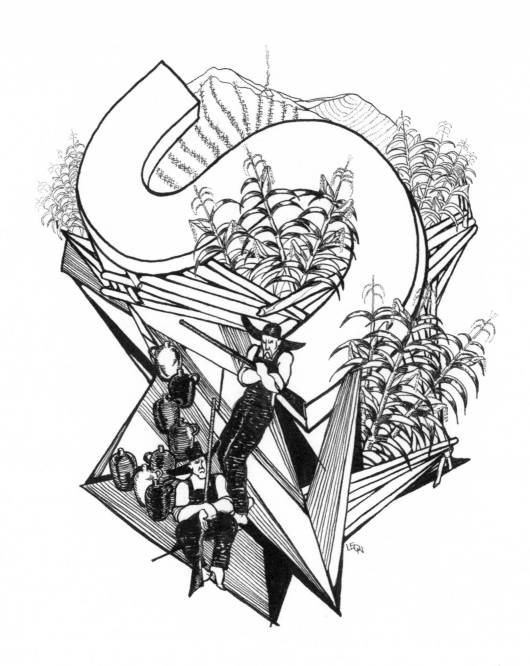

The humble, unobtrusive Still
    Protected by a man of will
Has, like the naughtylus of rime,[*]
    Expanded, until at this time
The tiny, unpretentious Still a
    Splendid easy speaking villa
Is—with lackeys left and lackeys right
    And carpets soft and richly bright,
While the protecting man so lone
    Has now the stature of Capone.
Big business can so quickly grow
    From small beginnings—Still and Slow.

STATISCOPE

3/4 Gin
1/4 Grenadine
Juice of 1/2 Lime
White of 1 Egg

SLOW MOTION

1 Pint of Corn[†] (from any State)
1/2 Pint of Cream
Whites of 2 Eggs
1 Tablespoon Grenadine
Add Vichy or Seltzer

---

[*] A reference to the poem "The Chambered Nautilus," by Oliver Wendell Holmes. As the nautilus grows, it builds chambered cells, each larger than the one before.

[†] pint of corn: corn whiskey or moonshine.

TST-TST!

Tiny words that suit the queasy,
  Vocalized in each speak easy
While the 1000 eyes of night
  Peep from out their slit holes slight,
How America rejoices
  In her soft, low Tst-Tst voices!

TST-TST

1/4 Pineapple Juice
1/2 Gin
1/4 Italian Vermouth
Few drops of Apricot Brandy

TAILSPIN

1 dash Orange bitters
1/3 Canadian Club Whiskey
1/3 French Vermouth
1/6 Lemon Juice
1/6 Grenadine

Ululating* Undertakers
Collecting relics from the shakers,
Stocks go up and stocks go down
Bears and Bulls go round and round
But the undertakers know
Spirit business is not slow.
So they ululate about
Getting those who're passing out,
Placing lilies on the shell
Of the ones who've lived too well.

ULLA LULLAH

1/4 Grapefruit Juice
1/2 Gin
1/8 French Vermouth
1/8 Italian Vermouth
Few Maraschino drops

---

*ululating: emitting a high-pitched howl or cry of lamentation.

The Vivandiere* of camp and tent
    Had boys along where'er she went.
So useful was this little creature
    Napoleon thought her quite a feature.
But now one need not go so far
    As battlefields or tents of war
To taste her most inviting wares
    For we have parlor Vivandieres!

VOLAPUK†

Juice of 1 lime
1 teaspoon Grenadine
2/3 Apple Jack
1/3 Gin

VACUUM CLEANER

1/3 Cognac
1/3 Porto Wine
1/3 Blackberry Brandy
1 yellow of egg

---

*vivandière: a woman attached to military troops to provide water and wine.

†Volapük: a language constructed in 1879–80 by Johann Martin Schleyer, intended to be an international language.

People who are really choosy
    Wish to know just who is whoosie!
Pedigree, the indicator
    In the Social Radiator,
Can be found by turning to
    The fateful letter—W

As important are the Whatsies
    To the people who have gutsies,
Whoosies who have lots of What
    Are the Whoosiest Whoosies—but
Whoosies Whats and Whatsies Whos
    All are under—Ws

WHATSIE

2 Glasses Whiskey
2 Glasses French Vermouth
2 Glasses Italian Vermouth

WHOOSIE

1/4 Cointreau
1/2 Gin
1/4 Sirop-de-Citron

X is the cross
　　That all of us bear
Cheerfully valiant
　　With stoical stare,
And faces quite Xanthic[*]
　　(complexion divine)
The color of Chartreuse
　　Of beer and of wine!

XX GRAND[†]

1 teaspoon Sugar
1 glass of Gin
Rind of 1 Lemon
Cubes of ice
Fill remainder of tall
glass with Ginger Ale
(This makes one entry)

And what a neck!

---

[*] xanthic: yellow.　　　　　　　　[†] "xx grand": ultra-fine sugar.

The Yaffle is the measuring line
Of your capacity and mine.
  The Yaffle that's enough for me
Scant indeed for you may be
  While the Yaffle you imbibe
Might suffer me to tack and gibe.
  Have you yaffled yet to-day?
Is the pleasant, courteous way
  To inquire with discerning
If the Yaffler still has yearning.

YAFFLE

1/2 Chamberi Vermouth
1/2 Bacardi Rum
Few drops of Grenadine

YAW-YAW

1/2 Lime Juice
1/2 Bacardi Rum
1 Teaspoon Sugar

The Babylonians always spent
Their time star gazing, as they went
　　From field of corn to field of corn;
For Babbleonions yet unborn
　　They plotted the celestial sky
So that, star gazing, you and I
　　Might read the Zodiac's signs and know
Just what they mean for those below.
　　First Sagittarius, hunter stellar
Emboldens us to find the cellar,
　　While the He Goat's capricious leap
Bids us to caper, not to creep.
　　Aquarius shows no keen enjoyment
In water bearing—odd employment,
　　The fish are not an idle couple
Because their bodies are so supple,
　　While ram and bull are unbelievers
In birth control—and gay deceivers

ZINGARO*

2 Dashes Orange Bitters	Squeeze lemon peel on top of
1/3 Port Wine	each glass before serving.
2/3 Gin	

---

*zingaro: a gypsy.

The heavenly twins appear to be
    And what they're doing—Gemini!
The crab has backward navigated,
    Example for the addle pated,
Leo delights to be rampant
    And pities anyone who can't;
The Virgin taking in the corn
    Makes wise provision for the morn
And Libra shows just how it came
    That night and day can be the same.
Large venomous reptiles in December
    The Scorpion bids us all remember!
So for each month there is a symbol
    To aid us in our antics nimble,
How thoughtful of old Babylon
    To give us these to ponder on
For every planet's odd position
    Is pertinent to prohibition!

ZAMBOMBA*

1/3 Absinthe
1/3 Anisette
1/3 Brandy

---

*zambomba: a drum.

APODOSIS[*]

IFS

For Hostesses

IF

You haven't a very large icebox electric
    And you wish to avoid a party that's hectic,
RING IN THE ICE MAN—and purchase some ice
    For hottentot cocktails are savagely VICE!

IF

Your strainer is old and its holes are not small
    Garbage it please— DON'T USE IT AT ALL!
The price of a strainer is not above rubies
    And many a seed has lodged in a booby's
Appendix—a booby who would not complain
    Of his hostess's strainer that never could strain!

---

[*] apodosis: see note for the letter L.

IF

You're mixing your cocktails be sure to beware
　　That you have enough liquor to amply take care
Of ice that is melting—else guests who come late
　　Will drink only stribblings—inexcusable fate!

IF

You wish to be known as a hostess parfait
　　Follow these does and these don'ts every day.

DON'T

Serve

Lettuce jumping sandwiches
Cakes of phenolactic complexion
Olive pest sandwiches
Fudge salad sandwiches
Soggy toast
Stale wafers

DO

Have the makings of highballs in the offing.
See that the olives wrapped in bacon are served hot.
See that weenie sandwiches are piping.
Supply your guests with the opportunity to make their own Tidbits.
(A cheese board is excellent for this purpose and also defers nittennotten).
Let your sandwiches be crisp and to the point.
Remember that fresh caviar deserves royal treatment.
Serve fresh caviar in a bowl surrounded by cracked ice
with chopped onion and lemon topping the caviar.
Let your guests spread their caviar—
(it is excellent work for the unemployed).
Have hors d'oeuvres appetizing and plentiful.
Shake your cocktails yourself unless you are sure of your butler.

Err always on the side of too much food rather than on that of too little.

ACKNOWLEDGMENTS

I would like to thank the descendants of Hilda Phelps Hammond, who made this project possible. I came to them out of the blue, and they each helped me. Thank you John Phelps Hammond Jr., Julie Hammond North Murphy, and Lilian Hammond Waterhouse.

I'm grateful to the cocktail historians who introduced me one to the other and for those who reviewed the recipes. Thank you Elizabeth Pearce, Ann R. Tuennerman, Philip Greene, Ted Haigh, and David Wondrich.